Secrets Of Successful Writing

Secrets Of Successful Writing

By Dewitt H. Scott

Edited by Sigrid A. Metson

Secrets of Successful Writing

Third Edition

Printed in the United States of America

ISBN: 0-9626212-1-8

Foreword from the Publisher

Reference Software creates writing improvement tools for people using personal computers. Our initial release was the *Random House* Reference Set—the first pop-up dictionary and thesaurus. Our next product was Grammatik, the first microcomputer software to proofread word processor files for grammar and style errors. The second release of Grammatik included *The World's Shortest Writing Course*, a book that taught people how to improve their writing using software tools.

Today, millions of people own personal computers. They are aware of software like Grammatik that will help improve their writing. The software provides convenient and accurate proofreading. Yet these people still have writing problems. Their difficulty is with basic writing techniques.

Good writing is the result of planning and sensitivity to the intended audience. It is concise, specific and uses fresh descriptions. Software can help identify and eliminate writing problems after they are on paper (or in a word processor file), but software can't conceive and plan for the writer.

When DeWitt Scott called me, I knew we had found the answer. He believes that writing that works is writing that communicates. We decided that a book like *Secrets of Successful Writing*, combined with a powerful proofreading tool like Grammatik, would help people convey their message more persuasively.

Secrets of Successful Writing complements Grammatik. It helps you improve your writing before you begin.

Keep this book by your computer. Refer to it constantly. Your writing will become more powerful and effective. In short, it will be more than correct—it will communicate.

Donald R. Emery, Ph.D.
President & C.E.O.
Reference Software International

Table of Contents

INTRODUCTION

TO WRITE WELL, you need only to get your ideas across simply and clearly. Most of us have something to share. I want to share my ideas on how to write simply and clearly. You want to share yours on the state of the world, the way your company should be run, 100 ways to cook hamburgers, your rare coin collection or whatever. If only, you say, I could tell other people what I know or persuade them to do something.

You can, if you:

- Respect your reader.
- Talk to your reader.
- Keep it simple.

To help you do that, I have tried to boil down the advice of good writers and editors to some tested guidelines. There are few rules in writing — many guidelines, but few rules. I have three rules: no blasphemy, no obscenity, no dishonesty.

It's no accident that the word *simple* appears so often in this book. I have three shelves filled with books about writing and word use. Some are excellent, good, or at least useful enough to keep. But they range from long to very long, and I believe many people want something short and simple.

Also, most writing advice comes from writers; this comes from an editor. I have been an editor for most of my 40 years in journalism. I enjoy boiling down showoff writing into language we can all understand, language that works.

To test how well my advice works on a composite "average reader," I showed these guidelines to a high school dropout, a history professor, an upholsterer, a civil engineer, a lawyer, a teacher, a farmer, a phone solicitor, a 14-year-old and an 81-year-old. All understood them. So can you.

Know Your Readers

PEOPLE ARE SMARTER THAN YOU THINK. There's no "typical reader," who will read no sentence longer than 15 words, or will read no more than five paragraphs of anything. That's insulting. Have faith in your reader and forget that "typical" nonsense.

Remember, I showed a draft of these guidelines to ten people, from the high school dropout to the college professor. Everybody understood it. Nobody thought it was too simple or too tough; nobody resented my tone. When you write, fix ten people of different types in your mind and "talk" to them — with respect.

At the same time, remember that most people read to obtain information. What you write for such people should address **their need** to get information quickly and painlessly. The average magazine or newspaper article is written at a sixth- to eighth-grade reading level. This doesn't necessarily mean that most people buying magazines have only a sixth-grade education or that the author writes only at the sixth-grade level. It just means that this reading level is sufficient to communicate most information.

Readability statistics are one measure of how effectively writing communicates. If you know your readers, readability statistics, like the Flesch-Kincaid Grade Level and Gunning's Fog Index, can help you adjust your writing to make it easier to understand. They identify what reading level your audience needs to understand your document. These statistics also offer clues to simplify your writing.

Computer writing tools like Grammatik automatically compute readability scores and provide instant advice on improving your writing. Suppose you're writing a proposal to obtain approval for an expensive telephone system. Your audience is a purchasing committee composed of employees with varying levels of education. After using Grammatik, you learn that the reading level required to understand your proposal is the 12th grade according to the Flesch-Kincaid standard. You also learn that the average paragraph in your document has sixteen sentences.

These statistics are telling you to take another look at your proposal. Why do you have so many sentences in each paragraph? Are you writing about more than one important point in each one? Could you make a more persuasive argument by letting each point stand alone? Would that make each point easier to read and understand?

Grammatik's statistics can't make these judgments for you, but they do give you an efficient way to gauge your work and tailor it to your audience. Use this information to create readable writing — it's what your readers deserve.

How To Begin

THINK IT THROUGH FIRST. Just as sloppy language begins with sloppy thinking, clear writing begins with clear thinking. A *Harper & Row* editor says, "Fuzzy thinking is the worst problem we find."

A professor won my respect when somebody asked a tough question. He started speaking, then said, "Let me stop talking a moment and think." He did, then answered clearly and well.

Thinking through a piece of writing involves three steps: unlimbering your mind, mapping out a beginning, a middle and an end, and focusing on your major point.

Your brain is an organ like your heart or lungs, and needs exercise. If you're a jogger, you do a few warmup exercises to unlimber your legs and get your blood circulating. If you're a tennis player, you volley for a while before beginning a match.

Do the same before writing. Just spew out gibberish, stream-of-consciousness, any words that pop into your head, especially clichés. It's called free-writing. Something like this maybe:

"Grandma got run over by a reindeer." Or this: "The lazy brown fox jumped over the underachiever and split his infinitive." Or whatever.

Wordplay serves at least three purposes: It wakes your brain and prepares it for action. It helps you discover what you think — sometimes you don't know what that is until you empty your brain and see what's up there. Wordplay also helps you to lighten up, to relax. To write well, to be comfortable with the language, you must relax.

The second part of thinking is working out a road map of where you want to go with your writing. To some writers, this means doing something like wordplay — just dashing off ideas as fast as you can, revising and organizing your thoughts later.

What works best for most writers is thinking through a beginning, a middle and an end — a structure. Ernest Hemingway said that "prose is architecture, not interior design."

You probably won't need the outline you learned in school — I, Ia, Ib, II, IIa, etc. — but you do need a road map of some kind, whatever works for you.

Much writing is about how to solve problems. Ordinarily, present the problem first, then the solution. By setting up the problem, you let your readers experience it. Then they'll read along through your efforts to solve the problem.

Every piece of problem-solving writing should have a point. "But it should also have a 'so what' — the reader's reason for reading it," say writers Susan Dellinger and Barbara Deane. They advise deciding on three "musts" before you write:

- What is this about? (The main point.)
- Why should my reader be interested? (The "so what.")
- What should my reader do about this? (The goal or purpose.)

As you gather confusing information, try to anticipate your reader's questions and quickly jot down the obvious ones. It's a good technique for organizing a long piece of writing.

Three-by-five cards may help organize your material. A *Reader's Digest* editor suggests writing on them — one point to a card — all the points you need to make. Divide the cards in piles, one pile for each group of points closely related to each other. (If you were describing an automobile, you'd put all the points about mileage in one pile, all the points about safety in another, and so on.)

Arrange your piles of points in a sequence. Which are most important and should be given first or saved for last? Which must you present early in order to make later ones understandable?

Now within each pile, do the same thing — arrange the points in logical, understandable order. There you have your outline, lacking only an introduction and conclusion.

To write this book, I did about the same thing on my outliner. Software that helps you outline is useful. Many advanced word processors come with outliners or you can buy them as stand-alone software. They're great. You just type in the key points in no particular order. You can even type in supporting points as you think of them. Once they're all on screen, it just takes a couple of commands to arrange them in a logical order. When you're ready to start writing, just press another key and you're working in your word processor (with its full editing capabilities) and all your important points are already on your screen.

My way to organize a piece of writing is to combine those little piles of information with a formula, either *1-3-2* or *2-3-1*.

Direct-mail copywriters use the *2-3-1* formula. They decide on two statistics, two quotations or two anecdotes that illustrate their message, the main idea in the letter. When they have chosen, let's say, two good quotes, they pick the second best for their beginning. They fill in the body of the letter with the rest of their quotes, statistics, facts and other information, strung out in logical order. Then they end with the best quote, the one that precisely makes their point.

Thus, *2-3-1*. Why? Because people remember best what they read last. Direct mail, popular in advertising because it works, makes its biggest selling point by ending with what copywriters call the "kicker" or "stopper." The P. S. on a letter may make its most important point.

It really doesn't matter all that much whether you lead off with your best or second best. They're both good; they're the best anecdotes, clever quotes, summary statements or statistics you have. What does matter is that they play off each other and that both "sell" your main point.

Most important: Your ending should be an echo of your beginning. If you close with a quote, it might grow out of the one you began with. If you opened with an anecdote — and that's often the best way to open — the closing anecdote should reflect the opener. But remember, whether you choose the *1-3-2* or the *2-3-1* or even the old *1-2-3* outline, your ending should echo your beginning.

You save yourself work with an outline. With it you can ask yourself about every fact, anecdote or quote you write: Does it relate to a point in my outline? If not, you're getting off the track (or else you've discovered another point you should have included).

The third and most important part of thinking is focus. Your report or letter may make many points, but it should focus on one main idea or theme. Editors sometimes tell writers to put story ideas into a headline of six to eight words, to be sure they have "a handle" on the story. The producer David Belasco told playwrights, "Unless you can write your idea on the back of a business card, you don't have a clear idea."

Every anecdote, statistic, quote, fact or bit of humor should help develop that idea. If it doesn't, throw it out. For years I tried to work this phrase into an article: faith, hope and clarity. It's clever, perhaps, but it made no point and I rejected it. Until now.

How To 'Talk' To Them

ONCE YOU HAVE FOCUSED your message on your readers, "talk" to them in conversational language. People often tell stories interestingly, then sit down with a pen or at a keyboard and tell the same stories dully. Why we have this double standard, I can't say, but it's there. I oppose it and urge you to do the same.

Conversational writing doesn't mean "talking" to people with low-brow or street language. Nor does it mean the scholarly talk at the faculty club. It means the language you use in serious conversation. It means using contractions and pronouns. It means using simple sentences, with active verbs that leave no doubt about who's talking to whom.

It means using direct quotations. People who lived an event can usually tell it better than you can, so let them do it, in their own words. But be wary of long monologues. If the quotes don't advance what you're trying to say, stick to your own words.

Listen to John Steinbeck, recalling his thought when he sat down to write *East of Eden* for his two young sons:

> *"Perhaps by speaking directly to them, I shall speak directly to other people. One can go off into fanciness if one writes for a huge, nebulous group."*

Consider Citibank of New York. It simplified its loan note wording by personalizing it with conversational language. The writer used active verbs, shorter sentences and contractions, and addressed the consumer directly. Listen to the words in Citibank's new section on co-makers:

> *"If I'm signing this note as a co-maker, I agree to be equally responsible with the borrower. You don't have to notify me that this note hasn't been paid."*

Consider also how an insurance company simplified a complex idea. Rather than write a long legal description of "restrictive purpose," the company took facts from an actual case to make a short, crisp example. Listen:

> *"Your teen-age daughter borrows a car belonging to her friend's father with the understanding that she's to drive to the airport. She's covered if she goes to the airport but not if she goes on a 400-mile trip."*

Conversational writing means using simple words. If you think you have to string together big words and fancy phrases, you're wrong. Your purpose is to explain something, not to prove that you're smarter than your readers.

Early in life, some of us develop a *double vocabulary* — simple words for speaking, longer ones for writing. We may say *he quits his job* and then write that he *resigned his position*. Or we say *about* and write *approximately*, or say *buy* and write *purchase*, or say *method* and write *methodology*. Use the simpler word, which immediately brings an image to mind. When you use the longer one, you force the readers to "translate" it through the simpler word before they see the image. Keep it simple.

Many Madison Avenue pros consider John Caples the best copywriter in the advertising field. Listen to him: "Sometimes you can change a word and increase the pulling power of an ad. Once I changed the word *repair* to *fix* and the ad pulled 20 percent more.

"Times change. People don't. Words like *free* and *new* are as potent as ever. The subjects that are new change but the human curiosity to know what's new doesn't."

Somebody, a copywriter probably, put together a list of the most persuasive words in the language. Not surprisingly, they're also simple words: *easy*, *yes*, *free*, *money*, *save*, *new*, *results*, *now*, *sale*, *health*, *benefits*, *safety*, *love*, *discovery*, *proven*, *guarantee* (and columnist L. M. Boyd slipped in one more — the hyphenated persuader: *time-and-a-half*).

Joe Girard calls himself America's greatest salesman and *The Guinness Book of Records* lists him that way, so listen to him. He advises using "move-forward" words and avoiding "hold-back" words. His move-forward list: *you*, *yourself*, *yours*, *we*, *our*, *ourselves*, *promise*, *please*, *thank you*, *excuse me*.

His hold-back list: *I*, *me*, *my*, *myself*, *late*, *maybe*. "These words usually indicate that you are communicating on your terms," he says, "and not on the other person's." At one big corporation it's a sin to use *I*, Girard says. "It's a rule that all letters it sends, from the president on down, cannot be mailed if they contain the word *I*."

I don't agree completely. *I* is direct and tells people, without pussyfooting, who wants or thinks something. And as for *we* writing, Mark Twain argued against it. He said, "Only kings, editors and people with tapeworm have the right to use the editorial *we*."

Conversational writing also means translating "tech"and other jargon. Tech is the language technologists — computer people, for example — use in talking to one another, shutting out the rest of us. Tech is OK between technologists, but it's not OK between technologists and us regular folk. Don't use words and expressions known only to people with specific knowledge or interests unless you are writing only for those people.

Listen to science writer Howard Levine: "Talking tech is what the public relations officer from the chemical plant is doing when he speaks of polychlorinated biphenyls in the food chain and what you really want to know is whether that stuff oozing from the ground will turn your kids into mutants."

Finally, conversational writing means being honest. Don't exaggerate or overstate. If your reader catches you once in an overstatement, every other point you try to make will be suspect.

Now you know conversational writing. You write with your ears more than your eyes. An editor I know suggests "wearing a blindfold and listening for good writing."

The Simple Sentence

THINK OF THE SENTENCE as a table with good lines, balanced on four sturdy legs. It works well until you start tinkering with it, shortening or lengthening its legs or adding some filigree here, a doodad there. Then it can come unglued or at least become unwieldy.

So can a sentence. Sometimes you get lost in a complex sentence and can't find your way out. I did in Chapter 2. At first I wrote the sentence this way: "Years ago a history professor won my respect when, asked a tough question, he started talking, then stopped and said, 'let me stop talking for a moment and think,' after which he answered clearly and well."

A few problems with this sentence: too many words — he "stopped talking" twice. Who cares whether he taught history or physics? What does "years ago" add? When you're trapped in an involved sentence, don't try to fight your way out. Start over again with a simple sentence — subject, active verb, object of the verb and period.

Try to limit each sentence to one idea or fact. You should vary the length of your sentences to avoid monotony but, generally, stick to one point per sentence. Look at these two versions: "The hearing, which began Monday, is the first step toward possible revision of the code, which the home construction industry considers essential to development but which critics call a tax giveaway." The 31-word sentence is correct but has three flaws: It's too formal; it's cluttered by four elements, and its vocabulary needs tightening.

You could shorten it to two or three sentences. Notice the easy pace and language of this version: "The hearing began Monday. It's the first step toward possible revision of the code. Home builders consider it essential to development but critics call it a tax giveaway."

To write simple sentences, speak simple sentences. For example, listen to a letter from the president of Command Airways to an aggrieved customer:

"Dear Mr. Kemp:

Clearly we screwed up. Please accept our apologies. Attached is a check for $168, which represents a full refund."

That's clear, and so is this, written a hundred years earlier by Cornelius Vanderbilt, the railroad man:

"Gentlemen:

You have undertaken to cheat me. I won't sue you, for the law is too slow. I'll ruin you."

Again, don't bury your most important point in the middle of a sentence. For better emphasis, put it at the end. It often works better at the end because people remember most what they read last.

In defining the simple sentence, my dictionary gives this example: "The boy ran home quickly." The working parts are the subject, "the boy," and an active verb, "ran."

A few words about the boy: When you add his age, address and grade in school to the sentence, you slow the action. When you write into the sentence *why* he's in a hurry, you slow it some more. And when you get fancy, add a buddy and clutter the sentence with punctuation and tangents, it begins running wild: "The boy, third-grader Roger ("Speedy") Smith of 115 Rapid Blvd., Grand Rapids — his friend Charley churning doggedly along beside him— ran home quickly because his mother had promised to spank him if he got home late."

That's complicated — and of course a silly example — but the point is simple. Give the boy running room. You do it by postponing the postponable details to the sentences that follow.

Backing into a sentence can add variety but can also slow it. For one more romp with the boy, you might be creative: "The memory of yesterday's spanking still fresh, the boy ran home quickly." So far, so good. It's less simple, but the sentence still works.

Or you might back into it this way: "Because his mother threatened to spank him for being late, the boy ran home quickly." This isn't clear. It suggests that she has just threatened him, when in fact she did it yesterday and he ran home quickly today. (Grammarians advise against beginning sentences with *because*.)

Here are a few more guidelines about writing sentences:

✍ Use lots of periods, the more the merrier. The period is your reader's best friend; it's like a life raft to a swimmer.

✍ Read the sentence aloud in one breath; if you can't, it's too long. Such a sentence is like a golfer's drive — if it goes too far it will land in the rough.

✍ The more complicated the subject, the shorter the sentences. Think of that when you're making a complicated legal point or explaining an involved tax matter. You might break it down into two or even three sentences.

✍ Apply the *2-3-1* formula. Remember the *2-3-1* outline? Write sentences and paragraphs the same way.

For example, note the *2-3-1* at work in this paragraph: "Don't bury your point in the middle of a sentence. For better emphasis put it at the end. That drives home the point because people remember best what they read last." That's three sentences starting with Number 2.

It works:

No. 2: Don't bury your point.

No. 3: Put it at the end of the paragraph.

No. 1: The why: because people remember best what they read last.

Thus, *2-3-1*.

I could have said the same thing in one *2-3-1* sentence: “Don't bury your point in the middle of a sentence, but put it at the end because people remember best what they read last.”

Besides driving home your major point, the *2-3-1* formula does something else: It builds in a natural transition that propels the reader on to the next sentence, to the next paragraph.

A word of caution about simple sentences. True, you should limit them to one point per sentence, usually, but vary the sentence length. The rhythm of writing depends first on the words, but also on a good mix of sentences — short, medium and even a few long ones that hold together well.

Here's one that did. *Newsweek* magazine said, in reporting on a big hit Carl Yastrzemski of the Boston Red Sox made on his 44th birthday, “It was the durable player's 1,839th career RBI, tying him with former Boston great Ted Williams, the very man Yastrzemski replaced in left field 22 years, five presidents, 451 home runs and 3,401 hits ago.”

Finally, a word in defense of the paragraph: Newspapers tend to string out one-sentence paragraphs, mostly for typographical reasons (to avoid great gray globs of type and create more white space). But the practice makes less sense now that columns are wider. Good writers think in paragraphs, not single sentences. The paragraph is the lever of solid thought; it makes sentences add up to rounded judgment.

To sum up: However you put together and string out sentences, keep them simple.

Be Specific and Precise

DETAILS KEEP YOUR WRITING ALIVE. Take Tolstoy's advice:

"I don't tell. I don't explain. I show."

Your words should call up pictures — colorful ones, preferably, the kind you sniff out like a good detective. To Jack Cappon, an Associated Press editor, "color" is a matter of details — often small, small details. Jules Loh of the AP, in a profile of Herbert Hoover, noticed that among many items on his desk was a tumbler with a dozen well-sharpened pencils — a detail most good writers would pick up. But Loh noticed also that the erasers on all the pencils were worn down. That detail told more about Hoover than all the obvious ones: the color of his necktie, the shine on his shoes, etc.

Colorful writing implies a way of *seeing* a story so you can *show* the reader. Wilson Thornley, a writing teacher, said: "Use your senses to gather concrete and exact information. Instead of saying a woman is 'nervous,' say instead that she kneads her fingers, that she slides her rings back and forth, working them over her knuckles, and that she chews on her lips."

Be precise. When you write, "Mary's mother says she can't go out Friday night," you raise a question: *Who* can't go out — Mary or her mother? Don't say "a period of unfavorable weather set in," say that "it rained every day for a week." And use *said* unless you really mean *revealed*, *stated*, *declared*, *argued*, *disclosed*, *asserted*, *claimed*, *noted*, *observed*, *pointed out*, *commented*. Each word has a specific meaning and shouldn't be used merely for variety.

A last word about being precise. Writers, trying to be fair, sometimes give up forcefulness and you don't know where they stand. I call it "on-the-other-hand" writing. Woody Allen put it well. "I do not believe in afterlife," he said, "although I am bringing a change of underwear."

BREVITY

"I AM SORRY TO HAVE WEARIED YOU with so long a letter but I did not have time to write you a short one," Blaise Pascal said. Tight writing is hard work and takes time.

Yet brevity isn't the end-all of writing. You get brevity by selection, not compression. When you're tempted to boil down all the information you have — to oversimplify — try instead to develop fully one anecdote or one point.

Some shortcuts waste your reader's time. Don't use "alphabet soup" abbreviations unless you're sure everybody will know what they stand for. Readers will know U.S., FBI, the U.N.; they might not know many others — ASCAP, for example. Use ASCAP only after you have said what it stands for: the American Society of Composers, Authors and Publishers.

William Zinsser, a writer and teacher, says, "Writing improves in direct ratio to the number of things we can keep out of it that shouldn't be there."

Writing, like a good manager, should be effective and efficient. In writing we can define these terms this way: *Effective* is saying the right things. *Efficient* is saying things right.

For a last word on the beauty of brevity, listen to the master, Professor William Strunk, in the *The Elements of Style*. "Vigorous writing is concise. A sentence should contain no unnecessary words, a paragraph no unnecessary sentences, for the same reason that a drawing should have no unnecessary lines and a machine no unnecessary parts. This requires not that the writer make all his sentences short, or that he avoid all detail and treat his subjects only in outline, but that every word tell."

"Sixty-three words," E. B. White said, "that could change the world."

Move Your Readers Along

SHORTENING — condensing — almost always makes your writing tighter, easier to understand and straighter. Here, your outline should save you work. If you did it right, your points already are in logical ABC order: A makes B understandable, B makes C understandable, etc.

To help the reader move along, don't just stack the facts; try to tell a story. Each sentence should lead naturally into the next without a lot of wordy transitional phrases. *In the meantime* and *on the other hand* are OK, but here are some better words to use when you shift gears: *now*, *later*, *today*, *still*, *across town*, *yet*, *nevertheless* — occasionally even *subsequently*, and *but* — yes, *but*, despite what they told you in grammar school.

Or *meanwhile*. It tells the reader you're changing moods, which you must signal right away. But the problem with *meanwhile* is overwork — and age. "*Meanwhile*, back at the ranch" predates TV to the time of radio serials. Newspaper writers abuse the word. They persist in patching together related stories and introducing each one with a *meanwhile*.

Or use *however*, to move the reader along. But don't end a sentence with the word because by then, Zinsser says, it has lost its *howeverness*.

When you begin a book, a chapter or a paragraph with *the* or *a*, it probably will be dull — or at least the first sentence will be.

Stay In Touch With People

PEOPLE WRITING MEANS TWO THINGS: writing about people and to them. An anecdote, a good idea or an abstraction will come alive if you introduce the person with the idea or explain how it affects people. Put flesh on people, quote them liberally and their ideas will come alive. *Time*, *Newsweek* and *People* magazines do this well.

So do advertising copywriters. Listen to Jerry Della Femina, an adman-author: "Young creative people start out hungry. They have just come off the street; they know how people think. And their work is great. Then they get successful. They make more and more money, spend their time in restaurants they never dreamed of, fly back and forth between New York and Los Angeles. Pretty soon the real world isn't people. It's just a bunch of lights off the right side of the plane. You have to stay in touch if you're going to write advertising that works. Ride a subway. Stand up on a bus. Buy a hot dog on the corner. Stay in touch."

Try to introduce people with their own words. Writer Tom Brady praises quotes (the writer's word for quotations) as "those brief, brilliant bursts of life."

When to quote people: when their words say it better than yours can, when you want to document or support a third-person statement, or to set off controversial material, or to capture a nuance or to convey some of the speaker's flavor.

When *not* to quote people: when the quoted words add nothing, as in: He called his job a "challenge" (a challenge is a challenge — a cliché maybe, but not worth quoting), and when the words make a point twice, as the following two sentences do: "He announced that the company would start the most ambitious development in its history. 'We'll launch our most ambitious development ever,' he said."

When in doubt about whether to quote or paraphrase, read it aloud to see how it sounds. The answer, usually, is whichever sounds more natural.

To write *to* people, involve them. This seems obvious, yet writers, especially of nonfiction, often miss the chance. You involve readers by using personal pronouns whenever possible (such as the *you* beginning this sentence). Opportunities abound, even in something as dry and straightforward as a do-it-yourself manual. Consider this sentence: "If the surface is scratched, its gloss can be restored with sandpapering and buffing." The sentence improves with a simple change: "If you scratch the surface, restore its gloss with...." If you're not sure who scratched it, rewrite it this way: "If you find the surface scratched, restore its gloss...."

Or "people" your writing with other personal pronouns: *she*, *he*, *herself*, *himself*, *their*, *them*, etc. Go through what you wrote sentence by sentence and look for the logical subject, the person (the doer) and not necessarily the grammatical subject. A long story about a new word processor mentioned, in the sixth paragraph, the engineers who developed it. The story could have let the *engineers* announce it in the next paragraph, then referred to it afterward as *their* processor, *their* development, *their* work. That's nothing dramatic, but by inserting a few *engineers* and *theirs*, the writer could have pointed up the human interest buried in the original story.

Almost any of *her, his* or *their* products, plans or ideas interest me more than a company's or a group's. If it comes down to a choice between people and things — and it often does — which interests you more? *Time* magazine writers average eight personal references for each hundred words. To uncover the ones in your writing, remember my guideline: think people.

PUNCTUATION

WHEN IN DOUBT, PUNCTUATE. When not don't.

The point, remember, is simplicity and clarity. If punctuation promotes them, fine; if it doesn't, leave the sentence alone.

Take the period (please — and often). Here's a story that might make the period more respectable. Twenty or so years ago, to prove his thesis that short sentences make writing more readable, a graduate student at the University of Illinois rated the readability of some newspapers, magazines and widely known writers.

He found the average sentence length of the tabloid *Daily News* in New York to be 19 or so words and the *New York Times* to be about 30 words. No surprise. Nor was he surprised to find that *Reader's Digest* sentences averaged a dozen fewer words than those in the harder-to-read *Harpers'* magazine. What did surprise him and many others was that three writers — columnist Ann Landers, World War II correspondent Ernie Pyle and Sir Winston Churchill — shared a sentence length that averaged 15 words. The popular Landers and Pyle didn't surprise people all that much, but Churchill did.

In 15-word sentences, Churchill's ringing wartime speeches in Commons rallied Britain. His blood-sweat-and-tears radio speeches rallied her Allies. His journalism from the Boer War until his death stirred the world. And he did most of it in sentences averaging 15 words.

So much for people who belittle the trend to short sentences as "see-Spot-run writing." The period is our best punctuation, period.

(That little "period piece," by the way, averages 15 words.)

The semi-colon — This may be the least-appreciated punctuation. It suggests a close relationship between two clauses; it helps to amplify a point; it signals contrast without the stopping power of a period; it nudges the reader onward with a pleasant little feeling of anticipation. It says: There's more to come; read on; it will get clearer.

The hyphen — Use it in compound adjectives: a two-car family, a high-level job, a 100-foot-tall tree, a 12-year-old daughter, a knock-down, drag-out fight (forget that one — it's a cliché). But don't use a hyphen after *ly*: a bad*ly* bent golf club.

The hyphen distinguishes like words from each other: recreation (fun) and *re-creation* (a remaking). And it clarifies: *A small-business man* runs a small business, but a *small businessman* could be either a midget or somebody you accuse of being petty.

The comma — This gets more use, abuse and overuse than any punctuation. Let's let it go with these guidelines:

Again: When in doubt, punctuate. When not don't. Consider, for example, how a comma changes the meaning of these sentences: "Do not break your bread or roll in the soup" and "Do not break your bread, or roll in the soup." (Common sense suggests that you rewrite the sentence.)

Use a comma to introduce a complete-sentence quote. "He laughed and said, 'She came back from London, after a week's vacation, with a British accent.'"

The colon — Use it to introduce quotations of more than one sentence. "He laughed and said: 'She came back from London, after a week's vacation, with an English accent. She had a great time.'" The colon's most frequent use is at the end of a sentence or a paragraph to introduce lists, tabulations, charts, etc.

You capitalize the first word after the colon when it begins a complete sentence. "She promised this: The company will make good on the employees' losses." But you don't capitalize the first word after the colon when it isn't a complete sentence. "She promised three concessions: making good on the employees' losses, rehiring the fired men and getting rid of the time clocks."

The dash — This signals an abrupt change of thought or an emphatic pause: "We will meet your terms — if our loan comes through — by the end of the month." And: "We will meet your terms — and they are terrible — because we want to end this matter."

Use dashes for a phrase that otherwise would be set off by commas, but which contains a series of words that call for commas: "He described the qualities — intelligence, initiative, assertiveness — that he wanted in a manager."

The exclamation mark — This suffers from overuse. It's often a vertical crutch holding up a weak sentence and insulting the reader. Save it for exclamations or commands:

> **A magnificent party!**
> **Ouch!**
> **Stop!**

When you use exclamation marks on lesser statements — "It was a great dinner!" — you gush. The *great* is gushy enough.

But, to repeat, the period is best of all. Use it often.

RECHARGE YOUR 'IONS'

NOW IT'S TIME TO LOOK AT *WORDS*, your principal tools, and *verbs*, your best tools.

I avoid nouns ending in *tion* and *ion*. I try to "activate" them (that means instead of *taking action*, I *act*). Those *ions* smother verbs, and verbs are the muscle of writing. They make a sentence move. You waste words when you *make a decision*; instead, *decide*. Activating verbs is an easy, often overlooked way to simplify and invigorate your writing.

Columnist Joan Beck calls verbs the vibrant heart of the sentence and says: "Verbs pump action into the message. They energize static nouns into motion and jab predicates into shape. Verbs tease, purr, shout, intrigue, hook, motivate."

Some verbs are tired. Fires "rage" on and on. Floods, battles and controversies "rage," too. Other verbs, especially solo uses of the verb *to be*, signal heavy going ahead: *am*, *are*, *is*, *was*, *were*, etc. You need them, of course, when your meaning calls for the passive voice. But be a verb activist whenever you can.

Before we go on, let's understand the terms. Active: "I *punched* the editor." Passive: "The editor *was punched* by me."

Besides *ion* and *tion*, look for these other endings that often smother verbs; *ing*, *ance*, *ment*, *ancy*, *ant*, *ent*, *able*. See how easily they convert to verbs:

To submit an argument becomes to **argue**.
It is the company's intention — it **intends**.
He offered an explanation — he **explained**.

She achieved dominance in her field — she **dominated** it.
They came to an agreement — they **agreed**.
The company realized a savings of — it **saved**.
They are in violation of — they **violate**.
Her contention was — she **contended**.
The panel reached a finding — it **found**.
They gave consideration to — they **considered**.

And so on; you get the idea. Remember that these are guidelines. When they work, use them; when they don't, don't. Sometimes you might want to say for effect that "she offered an explanation instead of "she explained." Go ahead.

When you think your writing is as "tight" as you can make it, look again. Look for *tion* and other endings that deaden the language — they are everywhere.

Lawyers and doctors in particular waste words with passive writing. Richard Wydick, a law professor at the University of California at Davis, argued the case for action verbs: "Cars collide. Plaintiffs complain. Judges decide. Defendants pay. Base verbs are simple creatures; they can't tolerate adornment. If you try to dress them up, you squash their life and motion."

Too many lawyers seem to ruin base verbs. *Collide* becomes *collision*, *complain* becomes *complaint*, *decide* becomes *decision* and *pay* becomes *payment*. Lawyers don't *act* — they *take action*. They don't *assume* — they *make assumptions*. They don't *conclude* — they *draw conclusions*.

Consider this sentence from a lawyer's letter (about overcrowding at California's San Quentin Prison): "Focus of a lawsuit would be on the overcrowded conditions there, together with the generally dilapidated condition of the institution. The goal of the litigation ideally would be the closure of the prison; alternatively, it would be a reduction of the institution's population."

Seven *tions* deaden the paragraph. Better: "A lawsuit would focus on overcrowding at the prison and its generally dilapidated state. The goal of the suit would be to close the prison, ideally, or to reduce its number of inmates."

Doctors tend to hide behind passive writing. To Dr. Nicholas Christy such writing "makes what you say impersonal, dignified and general. It has an official, formal and scientific tone." But what's really going on in the passive, he says, is that the writer "keeps action a convenient distance from the one who acts. I didn't do it. It wasn't me. It wasn't done. Magic."

Christy sampled three medical journals and counted the number of times the passive voice appeared in the first sentence of articles. In the *Journal of Clinical Endocrinology and Metabolism* he found the passive used 22 out of 25 times. In the *Journal of Clinical Investigation* the passive won 39 to 2. And in the *American Journal of Medicine* it was unanimous.

Prepositions (a *tion* I can't avoid) smother verbs, too. Instead of *coming upon* something, *discover* it.

Instead of *take hold of*, *grab it*. Instead of *putting up with* pain, *bear* it. And when you saddle verbs with *up*, you slow them further and also look silly: *Head up* adds nothing to *head* and *slow up* adds nothing to *slow*. Nor does *slow down*.

It may be hard to break the smothering habit, but try. Often these passive-to-active verb opportunities involve only two or three words:

"He has been scared by all of this Social Security talk." Better: "All of this Social Security talk scares him." "No fees were proposed by the committee." Better: "The committee proposed no fees."

Sometimes strung-out prepositions join the passive verbs in slowing the sentence: "The executive committee *of* the company voted *for* approval *of* the change, which will be ratified *by* the board *of* directors *at* its meeting *on* June 15." You can correct both faults — and get the time element with the verb — by rewriting the sentence: "The executive committee approved the change, which the directors will ratify June 15." That's 13 words instead of 27.

Often you can put life into an abstraction by "peopling" a sentence (Chapter 8) as well as "activating" it. Note how "the common reaction is incredulous laughter" comes to life with "most people just laugh with disbelief."

Often a pronoun and an active verb add touches of humanity that warm up your writing. Instead of, "The program was applauded by the board," make it, "Board members applauded *her* program." (You get the same personal touch when you say *his* project rather than *the* project, or *their* home rather than *the* home.)

Sentences beginning with *there was* or *there were* usually signal that you'd better back off and start again. Somebody wrote: "There was a similar plan introduced in 1982." Somebody rewrote it: "A similar plan was introduced in 1982."

Sometimes a sentence combines passive writing and a smothered verb: "Similar techniques were used successfully in Philadelphia." It tightens easily to: "Similar techniques succeeded in Philadelphia." Or again you could people it: "Doctors used similar techniques in Philadelphia."

And sometimes in the same sentence you can unsmother a verb, activate the language and people it. From a report about a pilot's "how-to" manual: "It provides information on what evasive action should be taken." Rewritten: "It tells the pilot what evasive action," or: "The pilot learns how to evade..."

A warning about "over-verbalizing." Computer people can access a central data bank, the dictionary says, but the rest of us should avoid this otherwise non-verb. That goes for some other *access* verbiage, too. When a State Department official reported that Salvadorans were taking advantage of a government amnesty offer, he said they had been *amnestized.* And Bill Walsh, then coach of the San Francisco 49ers, complained that their passing game had become *habitized.*

A last word about verbs: Whenever you can,

turn a negative into a positive. Instead of telling people what's "not," tell them what "is." For *did not remember*, say *forgot*. For *not honest*, say *dishonest*. For *did not have much confidence in*, say *distrusted*.

Enough. This probably labors the point, but it's an important one: Seeking active verbs is the best way to simplify and clarify your writing. So do it.

ADVERBS

SUDDENLY, BAD WRITERS are discovering adverbs, most of which just *ly* there doing nothing.

To begin with, avoid these sentence openers: *basically, typically, ironically, curiously, surprisingly, consequently, significantly, essentially, amazingly* and the cliché *hopefully*. Never mind whether *hopefully* is grammatical — which it usually is not — write it off as a cliché.

When you choose a verb that has a precise meaning and then add an adverb that carries the same meaning, you waste words: Radios shouldn't blare *loudly*, people shouldn't clench their teeth *tightly* and mope *dejectedly*. Of "*totally* flabbergasted," writer William Zinsser says, "I can't picture anyone being *partly* flabbergasted" — any more than a woman can be *totally* pregnant or *partly* pregnant.

In other words, adverbs are often redundant. Here are some of the more overused and abused adverbs:

currently and its near-twin, **presently** — When they follow the present tense, as in "she is *currently* writing a book" or "they are *presently* living in Chicago," they're redundant. In fact, the words are almost always redundant. Try this test: Every time you see *currently* or *presently* in a sentence, pluck it out and see whether you miss it. You won't.

clearly — A fact becomes no more evident when you make it *clearly* evident. Nor do incompetent people become more so when you label them *clearly* incompetent.

basically — You can forget it, and also *fundamentally* and *specifically*, unless you're writing about basics or fundamentals or specifying something.

arguably — It's a dumb, showy word. Forget it.

significantly — When you write that "the expense increased *significantly*," you say nothing except that it's noticeably (measurably) higher. Say how much higher.

meaningfully — This means to be "full of significance," which takes you back to significantly and where you were: nowhere with a nothing word.

absolutely — With this you add nothing to nothing and get nothing.

literally — Really? Truly? Consider the writer who informed us that a baseball team "*literally* pulverized" another, or the one who said the government "*literally* foamed at the mouth." Even though we know both are meant as figures of speech, they're silly.

virtually — Use it if you must, but consider what William Kerby, retired chief executive of the *Wall Street Journal*, said. In a memorable bulletin-board notice, he wrote, "From now on there will be *virtually* no *virtuallys* used in the *Wall Street Journal*."

immediately — It works well if you use it to get rid of junk like this: "at the earliest possible moment."

personally — Like *personal*, it's often redundant ("more than enough, overabundant, excess, superfluous, wordy"). When you say, "*personally*, I like it," you've said it twice. You can have friends, even close friends, but no "close *personal* friends." A statesman, commenting on the death of another one, once gave us a triple redundancy: "My own *personal* heart is breaking."

only — The trouble with *only* is the company it keeps — it gets lost a lot. It belongs with the word it modifies and winds up there only sometimes. Right: I have *only* one life to give to my country. Wrong: I *only* have one life to give to my country.

also — It's often redundant, as in "in addition, George is *also* going."

successfully — This, too, is often unnecessary. These appeared one week in three major newspapers: *successfully* withstand, *successfully* capture and *successfully* avoided.

very — Beware of purists who tell you never to use *very*. You should avoid it, true, but occasionally it can be effective (even if redundant), as in the hallmark of sloganeering: "when you care enough to send the *very* best."

simply — Years ago, in an English composition class, I used the word *simply* eight times in a paper. The professor sent it back with a note, "This simply won't do."

Simplicity speaks for itself. As Albert Einstein said, “Everything should be as simple as it can be, but not simpler.”

ADJECTIVES

LET'S NOT WASTE WORDS ON ADJECTIVES, which waste too many on their own. An editor once told me, half seriously, that I would need only three adjectives in writing: *a*, *an* and *the*.

Some work well: a *moist* handshake, a *crisp* presentation, a *green* thumb. Some don't: a *great* success, a *big* surprise, *green* grass.

Just as adverbs often add nothing to verbs, adjectives often add nothing to nouns. A problem with adjectives is that the idea is often already in the noun. So detour around those stately elms, gnarled oaks, towering mountains and precipitous cliffs. Instead, become a hard-bitten detective and sniff out all those yellow daffodils, lacy spider webs and sleepy lagoons. Your reward will be a friendly smile, maybe even a broad grin.

As Mark Twain said, "As to the adjective: When in doubt, strike it out." The secret to avoiding adjectives: Pick your nouns with care. Strong writing rests on choosing strong nouns and verbs.

LOADED WORDS

LOADED LANGUAGE PUTS PEOPLE DOWN, puts them off, puts them on and puts them out. There's no defense against some of it; a writer has to play it by feel. Pretend your reader is close enough to punch you in the nose. Some other advice that might help:

- ✍ Be yourself. Stick to language you know you know. Keep it simple. If it doesn't feel right, avoid it. By the time most of us pick up on *what's coming down*, it has come down and gone. If you're a middle-ager (unless you're Willie Nelson) don't affect the language of the young. You'll lose.
- ✍ Avoid stereotypes. "Getting rid of bias does wonderful things for writing," says Lucille DeView, an editor and writing consultant. "When we can't lean on stereotypes, we are forced to make descriptions more accurate and individual." Bias gets into writing even when we mean to praise: "The articulate black professor" implies that most black professors are inarticulate but this one is an exception. "The well-dressed Mexican children" implies that most are poorly clothed.

Of age stereotyping, DeView says: "Describing entertainer Hildegarde at one of her performances, at 74, as 'remarkably active for one of her age and anything but senile,' assumes that weakness is the norm in the later years. It is not. Only 5 percent of all people over 65 live in nursing homes, for example, although most stories about this age group are about this 5 percent."

These words and phrases demean, patronize or stereotype older people: *cute*, *sweet*, *dear*, *little*, *frowning*, *senile*, *old maid*, *fuddy duddy*, *Geritol generation*, *golden-agers*.

✍ Sexism abounds in writing. By now, we (male and female) know the kind of language that puts down women: *girl*, *coed*, *a blonde*, *man and wife*, a dozen *hims* for every *her* in an article, most words with *man* in them, labels like *pretty*, *vivacious* and *curvaceous* for her and *brainy*, *dynamic* and *assertive* for him.

To avoid the *he* and *his* problem in leases, loan agreements and other contracts, reword, and use the personal pronouns *you* and *we*. They "people" the document, sound less formal and "talk" directly to both sexes.

Or go plural, which may be the best solution. Suppose you begin a sentence talking about a person and then later use a pronoun to refer to that person. Should you use *he*, *she*, *him*, *her*, or what? It's a tricky problem and best solved by using plurals — *people* and *they*.

Some people defend using person as in *chairperson* for political — not linguistic or esthetic — reasons. Historian Ruth Schwartz Cowan explains why: "*Chairperson* is deliberately meant to fall awkwardly off the tongue because in its awkwardness it reminds us that persons in positions of authority may very well not be male."

Put another way, sexism isn't primarily a question of language, but of assumptions underlying language. Keep in mind that buyers, executives, defendants, lawyers, judges, doctors and officials are not exclusively male, and becoming less so. For *businessman* or *businesswoman*, you can easily substitute *executive* or *manager*. Instead of *man* and *wife*, make it *husband* and *wife*. Instead of *chairman* or *chairwoman*, make it *presiding officer, chair, leader, head, moderator*. A *salesman* can be a *salesperson*, a *sales clerk, sales representative* or *sales agent*. You can easily make *firemen firefighters, policemen police officers*, and *stewards* and *stewardesses flight attendants*.

There's more. Change the best *man* for the job to the best *person*. Change *man* or *mankind* to *humanity* or the *human race*, *manhood* to *adulthood, primitive man* to *primitive people*, and *workingman* to *worker* or *work force*. And the *average man* (whatever that is), or the *common man* or the *reasonable man* can be just an average, common or reasonable *person*.

In fact, we can all be reasonable about this. Two guidelines might help:

1) When you finish writing anything, if you're a male, ask a female to read what you've said. If you're a female, ask a male to do the same. Barring that, try hard to read what you've written through the eyes of somebody of the opposite sex.

   If you don't have a personal proofreader handy, Grammatik can proofread your documents for sexist language and provide you with tips on non-sexist phrasing. To check for sexist terms, just make sure Grammatik's Gender Specific Rule Class is turned on when you proofread your document.

2) If chairs and chairperson and personpower bother you, consider this: Extremism, in language as well as social action, must often precede social change. If you're secure in your own sexuality, all those chairs and all that power won't bother you.

A parting shot from feminist Gloria Steinem, speaking at Yale on language reform: "If the men in the room would only think how they would feel graduating with a '*spinster* of arts' degree, they would see how important this is."

Here are a few of the ways people trick one another — sometimes innocently, sometimes not. Use them sparingly if at all.

claim — To say "he *claimed* he had a reason" is to cast doubt that he did. With *claim*, you often hear a sneer or see a raised eyebrow. You *claim* something to which you're legally entitled. *Said* and *say* are fine little words — and fair, too — that usually do the job better. And they do it without calling attention to themselves.

elitist — This word sneers, too. It's a clumsy way of calling somebody a snob.

enhance — Remember when the right wine, a violinist and candlelight *enhanced* things? No more. Nowadays businessmen talk about "*enhanced* profits." The word means to intensify or heighten attractiveness; it doesn't mean simply to improve. When politicians talk about "revenue *enhancement*" they're soft-talking us — they mean higher taxes. And when military people talk about a "radiation *enhancement* device" they mean the neutron bomb, something to avoid.

forced — This, as in forced busing, began as the opponents' buzz word and news writers quickly adopted it. Call it *mandatory* busing.

free — The *free* world is no automatic synonym for the *non-Communist* world. Not all of the non-Communist world is *free*.

gossip — Maybe it is and maybe it isn't. If the report comes from Hollywood or elsewhere in show business, writers tend to call it *gossip*. But if they see something no better documented coming from Washington or Wall Street, it's *news* and sometimes *hard news*. Be careful with both gossip and the word itself.

liberal — Time has fuzzed its meaning. A few years ago Rep. Moris Udall decided to call himself a *progressive* although he really saw himself as a *liberal*. He did it because he said people associate *liberal* with abortion, drugs, busing, big spending, wasteful government and all that other bad stuff.

loophole — This sly word suggests devious or unethical behavior. Sometimes it's simply a tax advantage to which all of us — even rich business people or poor editors — are entitled.

qualified — Often this word is a smokescreen for racism and sexism, as in "the most *qualified* person for the job."

quality — "*Quality* health care" is a sickly phrase. It means different things to hospital administrators, Medicare doctors, overworked and underpaid nurses, patients and taxpayers. *Quality* education means one thing to a school superintendent, and something else to parents, to striking teachers and to the locked-out kids. As for *quality* food, housing and cars, they might just be expensive.

reform — This is as two-faced as any of the loaded words. Politicians love tax, prison, welfare, labor, abortion and even election *reform*. But the word means different things to different people. "Tax reform," as Senator Russell Long once said, means "don't tax you, don't tax me, tax that fellow under the tree." And welfare *reform* means one thing to poor people, something else to the wealthy and still something else to politicians.

self — You can learn a lot about loaded language — and about yourself — from studying the four columns devoted to *self* in your dictionary. The positives are fine — *self-control*, *self-examination* and especially *self-discovery*. But be careful with the negatives — *self-satisfied*, *self-appointed* and *self-anointed*. They sneer. If you're secure in who and what you are, you don't need to use words that sneer, ridicule or show off — that cover up, confuse or otherwise hurt people. If you look closely, you might find them self-serving.

so-called — Sometimes a word raises eyebrows and sneers at the same time. Consider, for example, how the word and the quotes combine to load this phrase: the *so-called* "gay rights" amendment.

sound, strong-minded — Maybe yes, maybe no. You and I are *strong-minded*, as you know, but *they* are opinionated, just as we have *vision* and they are *wild-eyed dreamers*. As columnist Sydney Harris said, "A *sound* man is one who sounds like me."

straightforward — It's a good word, but be careful with it. Somebody you find *straightforward* or *steadfast*, which suggest approval, may come across to others as *stubborn*, which suggests disapproval. You load the words when you refer to a president's course as *steadfast*. To others he might be *stubborn*.

type — A fem-lib *type* sneers and puts down a whole movement. So do a union *type*, a management *type*, the military *type* (not to mention the military *mind*).

totalitarian — Satirist Russell Baker, clarifying U.S. policy on human rights, explains that *totalitarian* states follow the Soviet line. But rights violators who follow the U.S. line — our free world partners — are *authoritarian* states. It depends on where you sit. If you're suspended by your thumbs in a *totalitarian* dungeon, the

U.S. government has a right to meddle but no power to help you. But if you're hanging by your thumbs in an *authoritarian* dungeon, "Washington has the leverage to get you out, of course, but that would be meddling, and the policy forbids meddling in *authoritarian* governments." A good rule of thumb: Avoid both *totalitarian* and *authoritarian* unless you're sure of your ground.

warn — *Say* and *said* are better substitutes here, too. *Warn* gives weight to empty words, especially a politician's, and implies a genuine danger or serious consequences that aren't there.

AVOID CLICHES

THE IDEA IS TO HAVE PEOPLE LAUGH WITH YOU, not at you. One night at a party, an engineer slyly asked an editor: "Which is highest— skyrocketing, astronomical or double-digit inflation?" His question suggests that it's long past time to retire all three clichés.

Some of the problems with clichés:

- We've seen so many of them for so long that we no longer recognize them as they limp by.
- Writers become comfortable with them. *Controversial issue* is a lazy writer's shorthand. It's a catchall to put a person or an issue under a cloud without giving your readers the details to judge for themselves.
- We don't always agree when a cliché is a cliché. Sometimes they bounce in — like *out of sight*, which already is, and *uptight* — and hang around long after they have lost their bounce. They were trendy words, and like *trendy* itself are now clichés.
- Quotation marks don't make them respectable. Let's say you're in a hurry and dash off "out of sight," cliché or no. When you wrap it in quotes — so the reader will understand that you know better — all you've done is call attention to the dumb thing.
- It's human to pretend we're experts. Jargon (specialized clichés) gives us such terms as *developmentally disabled* that sound impressive. A quick survey of eight editors and specialist writers found none who could say for

sure what it means, but five thought it had "something to do with retardation." The point: Define or explain it, or forget it.

I play a game that helps to weed out clichés — I give them a personality. You might want to consider briefly the Stumbling Blocks, a big tribe that began with klutzy old Chief Stumbling Block. It continued down through his heirs, the principal Stumbling Blocks, and thrives today under a major Stumbling Block. He and his fellow officers — the aggressive Major Breakthrough, the forthright Major Thrust and the generous Major Contribution — all serve under General Consensus. Silly, yes, but it works.

Here's a challenge for you. Try truly to write for a week — memos, proposals, reports, letters — without using one of these old hacks (from a collection by writing teacher Roy Peter Clark):

The right to a fair shake
The lion's share
We have no earthly idea
Before we rush headlong
We want to draw the line
Let's keep all avenues open
We can close the gap
That's a pretty big if
By the same token
A far-reaching effect
Moved to greener pastures
It's a step forward
There's a 50-50 chance
Grappling with the question

Caused quite an uproar
Don't want to rock the boat
Get the ball rolling
Pick up the tab
Swept under the rug
Looking over his shoulder
It remains to be seen
The cold facts are
In for rough sledding
It can't be established overnight
A sense of direction
An outspoken critic
It's being bandied about
Keeping the lid on
Moving to head off the problem
When the dust settles
A callous disregard for
So much excess baggage
The handwriting on the wall
The powers that be
Caught in a squeeze
It has to be ironed out
As a last resort
Get their money's worth
It seems to boil down to
Gets a lot of mileage out of
It has fallen on deaf ears
Fly in the face of
Wrestled with the question
Laid the groundwork
By any stretch of the imagination
Just in the nick of time
May throw light on the subject
This insults the intelligence

METAPHORS

WHEN THEY WORK WELL, METAPHORS (a figure of speech containing an implied comparison: *the curtain of night, all the world's a stage*) enrich the language. So do similes (also figures of speech, but distinguished by *like* and *as*, etc.: *a heart as big as a whale, tears flowed like wine*).

Jimmy Carter found eloquence in his farewell address about the nuclear shadow under which we live: "Our minds have adjusted to it, as after a time our eyes adjust to the dark."

When metaphors don't work — which is often — people laugh at you. Listen to Donald Nixon, brother of the former President, on Watergate: "It's unfortunate that what happened, happened, but people are using this as a political football to bury my brother."

And listen to *U.S. News & World Report*, not usually comfortable with colorful writing: "The economy haltingly emerged from the recessionary forest last summer but now seems stalled on the outskirts and could even inch back into the woods."

I tend to remember best the metaphors that don't work — and so will your readers: "Don't bite your chickens before they hatch," a Louisiana legislator advised, and also this, "To hell with posterity, what's posterity ever done for us?"

Joe Garagiola threw us a screwball: "Nolan Ryan is pitching a lot better now that he's got his curve ball straightened out."

A sports writer reported that "450 fishermen have been jammed on the pier like a can of sardines."

An unidentified businessman decided that "it's a matter of whose ox is being goosed."

Yet metaphors are useful. At their best, they can help us visualize an abstract idea. When the phrase *garbage in, garbage out* (GIGO) caught on, people began to lose their awe of the computer. In other words, it would do only what you told it to do with what you gave it.

Metaphors and similes can drive home a point — or several points — as historian-writer Barbara Tuchman did: "Let us beware of the plight of our colleagues, the behavioral scientists, who by use of proliferating jargon have painted themselves into a corner — or isolation ward — of unintelligibility. They know what they mean, but no one else does."

Metaphors can take us to the scene. In *The Monkey Wrench Gang*, Edward Abbey did it with words worth a thousand pictures: "*...the pure and brainless fury* of tons of irresistible water crashing down upon tons of immovable limestone." And again, a few pages later: "The great machine (a huge earthmover) *began to bleed*; its *lifeblood drained* out with *pulsing throbs*, onto the dust and sand."

Or metaphors can be just good writing, as is this by Norman Cousins, former editor of *Saturday Review*. "Whoever and wherever he is, the wordsmith likes the clink and purr of words against each other. He likes the crackle of ideas well expressed. He delights, as some men do in thoroughbred horses and racing hulls, in prose that runs sleek and true to its conclusion."

The problem with metaphors is that, like *crystal clear*, they often begin life with promise and end as clichés.

A last word about metaphors, from the AP's Jack Cappon. He calls metaphors sprinters, not long-distance writers, and says you have to know when to let go. He gives this example of a writer who doesn't know:

"Smith, an avid sailor, has been at the helm of his company five years, and during that time has steered it past many shoals. The worst squall he faced was a bitter proxy fight, but he weathered it and the seas have been calm since. In fact, the only one who makes waves now is Smith himself."

By the third sentence, Cappon says, the reader needs a life preserver.

SHOWOFFS

EVERY YEAR HAS ITS *BIG WORD*, which people then proceed to beat to death. Here is my current list of vogue words and showoffs: *ambivalent*, *bottom line*, *charismatic*, *communicate*, *dialogue*, *dynamics*, *feedback*, *hopefully*, *incredible*, *input*, *interface*, *knowledgeable*, *massive*, *meaningful*, *parameter*, *perception*, *relevant*, *share*, *system*, *thrust*, *viable*.

Should you use these words? Yes, but correctly and sparingly, and with the knowledge that good writers generally avoid them. The point is that abuse and overuse cheapen good words.

For example: Sex appeal, a nice smile and votes don't automatically make a politician *charismatic*. A few cars backed up on a freeway don't always add up to a *massive* traffic jam. And *communicating* is an art few people ever master — even those of us in communications. It combines the gifts of reading as well as writing; it combines those of listening as well as talking. It does not mean delivering a monologue well.

Once a writer referred to California's San Joaquin Valley as an area "where farming is *economically viable*." But why, when it can be so easily simplified to "where farming pays."

Edward Thompson of the *Reader's Digest* tells about the scientist who wrote, "The biota exhibited a one hundred percent mortality response" when he could have written, "All the fish died."

Consider the showoff, *parameter*. Paul Woodring, a teacher-writer-editor, says of it: "After its introduction a few years ago, *parameter* suddenly appeared in many publications where it was misused to mean limits or boundaries — perhaps because it sounds like *perimeter*. In fact, *parameter* is a very specific statistical term defined as 'a variable entering into the mathematical form of any distribution such that the possible values of the variable correspond to different distributions.' You may as well forget that — if you mean boundaries, say boundaries."

You won't find *parameter* at the U.S. Commerce Department. Soon after taking over as secretary of commerce, Malcolm Baldrige fed *parameter* and lots of other junk into his department's word processors and banned them. If a careless bureaucrat slips, the machine will stop and flash, "Don't Use This Word." In addition to *parameter*, the words and phrases he banned include:

- I would hope, I would like to express my appreciation, as I am sure you know, as you are aware, as you know, at the present time, best wishes;

- Bottom line, delighted, different than, enclosed herewith, finalize, glad, great majority, happy, hereinafter, hopefully, however, image, input, institutionalize;

- It is my intention, maximize, meanwhile, more importantly, needless to say, new initiatives, ongoing, orient, personally reviewed;

- Prior to, prioritize, serious crisis, share, subject matter, therein, to impact, to optimize, untimely death, very much, viable;

✍ I share your concern, contingent upon, effectuated, inappropriate, management regime, mutually beneficial, responsive, specificity, thrust, utilize.

That's a good hit list for anybody, in Washington or anyplace else. Why not make it your hit list?

On the other hand (there's always an *other hand* in discussing words), the language changes, and should. Webster's Ninth New Collegiate Dictionary lists 11,000 new words, including these that mirror changes in our ways of living and working: *survivalist* ("one who views survival of a catastrophic event as a primary objective"); *domino effect, biohazards, high tech, down-sized, weatherized, condo, hot tub, video games, genetic engineering, gene-splicing, bioethics, laid-back, palimony, open marriage, parenting, house husband, microchip, floppy disc, megabyte, electronic mail, petrodollars, gas guzzler*, and even these: *pig out, humongous, scuzzy* and *wacko*.

To be considered for inclusion, a Webster's editor says, a word must have proved itself for at least two or three years and have been used by a number of sources.

Lawyers, doctors and educators give us professionalese, bureaucrats give us bureaucratese and technologists give us computerese. When writers pass this stuff along they commit at least two crimes: 1) parrot-phrasing, and 2) perpetuating elitism — among lawyers, bureaucrats, technologists, educators, economists, doctors or any other group.

Economist John Kenneth Galbraith argues the case against elitism: "There are no important propositions that cannot be stated in plain language. The writer who seeks to be intelligible needs to be right; he must be challenged if his argument leads to an erroneous conclusion and especially if it leads to the wrong action. But he can safely dismiss the charge that he has made the subject too easy. The truth is not difficult. Complexity and obscurity have professional value — they are the academic equivalents of apprenticeship rules in the building trades. They exclude the outsiders, keep down the competition, preserve the image of a privileged or priestly class. The man who makes things clear is a scab. He is criticized less for his clarity than for his treachery."

Some educated people tend to use language that sounds elegant, to write complicated sentences and, in short, to show off. Some barely educated people do the same thing.

Alan Siegel, a business-writing consultant, makes a case for simplicity: "We're not trying to turn English into a language of one-syllable words. We're not even trying to do away with professional jargon, though that's always a tempting target. Let lawyers talk to lawyers, or accountants talk to accountants, or civil servants talk to civil servants as they please. As long as they understand each other, fine.

"But when lawyers, or accountants, or others are talking to a broad audience and demanding to be understood, then let them speak plainly and simply. When non-experts are forced to use certain documents every day, and are held responsible for understanding them, then those documents should be written for non-experts."

Simplicity sounds great in a world where language is changing faster than ever before. One big problem is the quantity of information you have to deal with. Like bad golf habits, bad writing habits are hard to unlearn. Showoff writing is especially hard to monitor in other people's work.

One way to increase your vigilance without adding to your workload is to create your own electronic style guide with Grammatik. The value of a custom electronic style guide is that

1) it is as easy to use as a spelling checker

2) it can reflect the special goals of your business

3) it's easy to modify.

Suppose you want all the letters from your company to use the word *client* instead of *customer*. Or suppose you are like Hewlett-Packard and want the abbreviation of your name (*HP*) to be used only as an adjective (as in *HP Service Office*) and to be written the same way every time it is used (as opposed to *H.P.* or *H-P* or *H/P*). Making a rule that tells Grammatik to flag the undesirable abbreviations and suggest the substitution *HP* is easy to do with Grammatik's Rule/Help Editor.

Once the rule is made, Grammatik automatically checks every document to make sure this rule is observed. That's much easier than keeping a huge list of appropriate terminology tacked to your bulletin board, or flipping through a hefty corporate writing style guide. It also ensures that everyone is writing using the same standards and that contributes to your company's image.

Little Slips

NOW, AS YOU STRING THE WORDS TOGETHER, be careful. Whenever I see any of a dozen errors — little slips and some not so little — they suggest that the writer is uncomfortable with the language, and I become uncomfortable with the writing.

Columnist James Kilpatrick puts it another way:

"If a reader keeps tripping over strange words, or bumping his head on overhanging clauses, or stubbing his toe on concealed antecedents, he tends to give up. The hell with this, he says, and he turns to something else. Our concern here is not with pratfall prose. It is the imperceptible hesitation that matters — the little uncertainty, the small confusion, the modifier that isn't badly lost but only slightly misplaced."

Here are the dozen slips to watch out for:

dangling modifiers — "A manager of great promise, the directors gave him some of the choicest business opportunities." The opening phrase appears to modify directors; the next word after promise should be *he* or *she*.

a misplaced modifier — "It's hard to understand why parents are reluctant to take their children to the police with drug problems." To make it clear, *with drug problems* belongs after *children*.

wrong word — "They convinced him to go along with the deal." No, they *persuaded* him *to* go along, or they *convinced* him *that* he should.

subjects and verbs don't match — "After the executive committee meeting, the chairman said the time, date and place of the convention *has* yet to be set." The subject is three things — the time, date and place — so write *have* yet to be set.

subject-verb problem — "The reason you brought your car in for was not corrected." *Reason* wasn't *corrected* is of course silly. The writer let himself get off the subject.

missing word — "He maintained the building was unsafe." He maintained *that* it was unsafe. Without the word *that*, for an instant ("the imperceptible hesitation") he looks like a maintenance man.

a missing comma — "Smith, another one of our executives is licensed as a CPA." *Another one of our executives* is a non-essential phrase that can be dropped without changing the basic meaning of the sentence. Set off such phrases and clauses with two commas. Another missing comma: "After the car hit the pole, she said the lights went out." To make clear when she said it and when it happened, you need the second comma after *said*, and quote marks after *pole* and before the *lights*.

misspellings — When people read *Noble laureate* for *Nobel laureate*, they have to question the writer's intelligence, education and everything else he has to say. This may not seem logical or fair, but it's the way it is. So my list of "little slips" includes these often-misspelled words: *accom-*

modate, acknowledgment, anoint, battalion, calendar, canister, cemetery, collectible, discernible, embarrass, fiery, guerrilla, harass, hemorrhage, inoculate, judgment, liquefy, minuscule, occurred, parishioner, permissible, promissory, rarefied, restaurateur, sacrilegious, seize, siege, sizable, supersede, weird.

My guideline: Instead of asking somebody how to spell a word, look it up. That will help fix the word in your mind. You can check your word processor's spelling dictionary faster than you can say, "Don, how do you spell *accommodate*? Is it one *m* or two?"

a misplaced word — "He said he would only be there for a day or so." *Only*, probably the most-often-misplaced word in the language, belongs after *for* — "for *only* a day or so."

sentence should be parallel — This one isn't: "The general manager suggests banning first-class air travel and rejection of expenses that exceed $100 a day for all executives." It must be either *banning* and *rejecting* or *a ban on* and *the rejection of.* Parallel, in this case, means using the same verb forms.

a missing apostrophe — "Any staff member can take the test, but *its* nearly impossible for anybody to get a perfect score on it." *Its* should be *it's*, the contraction for *it is.*

first/largest/most/longest/only — Well, maybe it's the *longest* drought, maybe it's the *largest* personal settlement ever and maybe she's the *only* woman ever to drive a steamroller in Brazil. And maybe not. It's best to give the beginning and ending dates of the drought and, if you must, say that it's *probably* the largest settlement or she's *believed* to be the only woman to drive a steamroller. But why bother? Besides being wrong, those *firsts*, *largest*, *mosts*, *longest* and *onlys* are often clichés.

FIGHTING CLUTTER

CHAPTER 4 BEGAN WITH A PLEA for clear thinking.

Remember the *Harper & Row* editor who said, "Fuzzy thinking is the worst problem we find." He added, "followed closely by clutter." To writing teacher William Zinsser, "Fighting clutter is like fighting weeds — the writer is always behind. New varieties sprout overnight and by noon they are part of American speech."

To fight clutter, make every word work. Instead of *in the majority of instances*, say *usually*. Take the word *personal*, as in a "*personal* friend of his" or "his *personal* physician." Nine times out of ten it's a throwaway word. Or take two other words — *both* and *different* — that are almost always padding. When you write that "Smith and Jones *both* passed the test," you add a weed into formerly uncluttered garden. When you write that "the ruling applies to several *different* cities," you do the same. Nobody has cloned a city. Or consider what somebody wrote about Norman Mailer: "He has had nine *different* wives." Perhaps that's better than having nine wives who are the same.

The word *between* clutters writing when used this way: "It will take *between* six and ten years to finish the work." Say instead that "It will take *six to ten* years to finish the work."

Little qualifiers also clutter the language: a *bit* tired, a *little* annoyed, *sort of* confused, *somewhat* puzzled. Forget them; go ahead and be confused.

"Paper-clip expressions" clutter it, too. That's what writing teacher Janet Larson calls these showy substitutes for ordinary prepositions: *in relation to*, *as it relates to, having to do with, in the process of* and the worst offender: *in terms of.* These look silly: the cost, *in terms of money*, the altitude, *in terms of feet*, congressional volume, *in terms of legislation passed.* They say nothing, which was probably what the writer had in mind.

When lawyers and others talk or write about "acts of a hostile *character*" and "acts of a hostile *nature*," they mean "hostile acts," period. When you're tempted to write about *conditions*, *situations* and *activities*, take a second look. Bad weather *conditions* are just bad weather, an emergency *situation* is an emergency and recreational *activities* are recreation, or just fun.

Clusters of prepositions clutter writing. With a little effort on the part of the writer of this sentence, he cut the clusters of prepositions in short order. And he wrote: Avoid clusters of prepositions.

Some verbs, even the shortest of them, can clutter the language. *Am*, *is*, *are*, *was* and *were* — any solo forms of the verb *to be* — deaden a sentence, said my first editor (and a dozen others along the way). He was and they were right, mostly.

Here are a half-dozen showoffs followed by short substitutes (in bold-face type), good words that do the job without calling attention to themselves: numerous for *many*, facilitate for *ease*, remainder for *rest*, initial for *first*, implement for *do*, sufficient for *enough*.

Consider how much better each of the following reads without the redundant words (lighter type):

Plans for the future
She was modest about herself
The general **public**
He owns his own **home**
Strangled to death
Jewish **rabbi**
A new **record**
Face up to **the problem**
Nodding his head
Shrugging her shoulders
Connecting **links**
Prior **notice**
Crime activity
Past **experience**
Easter Sunday
New **developments**
End **result**
He thought to himself
Contributing **factor**

Consider a few other redundancies: *meaningless gibberish*, *awkward dilemma*, *true facts* and *violent explosions*. To rid yourself of them, try turning them around. Can gibberish be meaning*ful*? A dilemma *pleasant*? A fact *un*true? An explosion *gentle*?

Blame lawyers for another kind of redundancy that clutters the language: doubletalk. It includes such near synonyms as *null and void*, *aid and abet*, *sum and substance*, *irrelevant and immaterial*, *part and parcel*. When you come upon them — and you will — see whether one word or the other doesn't say it all. That goes also for these: *bits and pieces*, *nook and cranny*, *safe and sound*, *ready and willing*, *fair and just, bound and determined, shy and withdrawn, various and sundry,* and *clear and simple.*

Still, many *clear* and *simple* words unclutter the language. *About*, for example, allows you to throw out all of this junk: *in connection with, with regard to, with reference to, with respect to, on the magnitude of, in the neighborhood of, a ballpark figure* — or even *approximately.* (A judge I know fines lawyers a quarter whenever they say *approximately* instead of *about* in his courtroom.)

Another fine word, *most*, allows you to fire these; *a large percentage of, the vast majority, the great majority, a significant majority, the overwhelming majority.*

Clutter is imprecise. Some dishonest people use it for just that reason. Consider a *goodly* share. What is it? Probably a bit more than *fair-to-middlin'* and a bit less than the *lion's share.*

Some of these junk words work. In conversation they're often, or can be, the glue that holds a sentence together or fills in lulls. But in writing most are dumb, wooden words that stand around doing nothing. These might get by in conversation, but they look ridiculous on paper:

Clutter	***Better***
the fact that	that
made up his mind	decided
personnel	people
prior to, in advance of	before
best of health	well

Clutter	*Better*
in the final analysis	finally
the foreseeable (or near) future	soon
on the part of	by
address the problem	face the problem
with the exception of	except
the absence of	no
the question as to whether	whether
draw your attention to	show you
in the event of	if
in order to, for the purpose of	to
a man by the name of	named
filled to capacity	full
in spite of the fact that	although
the month of August	August
put in an appearance	appear
positive growth	growth
in view of	because
at present, at this time	now
in short supply	scarce
in the majority of instances	usually
a percentage of	some
a large percentage of	most
was unaware of the fact that	didn't know
since that particular time	since then
did not remember	forgot
in a hasty manner	hastily
ahead of schedule	early
accordingly	so
there is no doubt that	undoubtedly
in attendance	there
from her point of view	to her
will have to	must
each and every one of us	each of us

Enough. I could fill a book with this stuff (and some people have). To the *Wall Street Journal,* clutter is "the criminally inane," and to George Orwell it's not just a nuisance but a deadly tool wielded by writers who want to hide the truth.

To Professor Strunk, weeding out clutter is what writing is all about. Listen again to his famous 63-word essay:

> *"Vigorous writing is concise. A sentence should contain no unnecessary words, a paragraph no unnecessary sentences, for the same reason that a drawing should have no unnecessary lines and a machine no unnecessary parts. This requires not that the writer make all his sentences short, or that he avoid all detail or treat his subjects only in outline, but that every word tell."*

MISUSED WORDS

NOW FOR THE GOOD WORDS that people often confuse, misuse or otherwise abuse. Dictionaries disagree on many fine points in the language, on what's acceptable and what isn't, so some of the distinctions are a consensus of people who use words well:

adverse, averse — *Adverse* means unfavorable. *Averse* means unwilling or reluctant.

affect, effect — Generally, *affect* is the verb (to influence) and *effect* is the noun (result). "His warning didn't *affect* our decision." "The warning has no *effect*." But *effect* is also a verb meaning to bring about: "It's hard to *effect* change."

alternative, alternate — Use *alternative*, as an adjective, for a second thing or something you propose for a choice. *Alternate* as an adjective means "occurring by turns," as "on alternate days."

anticipate, expect — Use *anticipate* when you mean looking forward to something with a foretaste of the pleasure or distress it promises. Use *expect* in the sense of certainty or confidence that it will occur. *Anticipate* a reunion, *expect* the sun to set.

bus, buss — *Bus* is a vehicle and the other a half-hearted kiss.

capital, capitol — Usually the word you want is *capital*, which means the city or the wealth or the upper-case letter; the other is the building.

compared to, compared with — Use *compared to* when you say that two or more items are similar. He *compared* his civil rights work to the campaign of Susan B. Anthony for women's suffrage. Use *compared with* when you juxtapose two or more items to illustrate similarities or differences. He finished in nine days, *compared with* eight for his rival.

compose, comprise — *Comprise* means to embrace. It takes X, Y and Z to *compose* a whole, but the whole *comprises* (embraces) X, Y and Z.

cope — You don't just *cope*, you *cope with* somebody or something.

demolish, destroy — They mean to obliterate ("to blot out or erase without a trace") so it's redundant to say you *completely* demolished or destroyed something. It's all or nothing.

disinterested, uninterested — *Disinterested* means unbiased or impartial. *Uninterested* means bored or indifferent.

dived, dove — The verb is *dived*; the other is a bird.

ecology, environment — They aren't synonymous. *Ecology* is the study of the relationship between organisms and their environment. *Environment* simply refers to our surroundings.

emigrate, immigrate, migrate — *Emigrate* refers to leaving a country. *Immigrate* refers to arriving in a country. *Migrate* means to change location (as birds do every winter).

farther, further — Use *farther* for distance, *further* in the sense of additional or continued.

flout, flaunt — *Flout* means to mock, scoff, show disdain. *Flaunt* means to display ostentatiously, to show off.

forbear, forebear — *Forbear* means to avoid or shun; the other is an ancestor.

forego, forgo — *Forego* is to precede. *Forgo* is to do without.

imply, infer — The speaker or writer *implies* when she makes a suggestion, and her listener or reader *infers*. She makes an *implication* and you draw an *inference*.

it's, its — *It's* is the contraction of *it is*; *its* is the possessive. (Try to "uncontract" it in your mind. Hint: An apostrophe often indicates that a letter or letters has been left out.)

jibe, gibe — *Jibe* means to be in harmony, or to shift the mainsail boom of a ship from one side to another. *Gibe* means a taunt.

lay, lie — *Lay* means to put or deposit, and requires a direct object. *Lie* means to be in a reclining position, or to be situated, and takes no direct object.

leave, let — To *leave* alone means to depart from or cause to be in solitude. To be *let alone* means to be undisturbed.

lend, loan — Avoid *loan* as a verb; use *lend.* Why? How does "Friends, Romans and countrymen, *loan* me your ears" sound to you?

mantel, mantle — *Mantel* is the shelf and the other is a cloak. To keep them straight, remember that you put your *el*bow on the mant*el.*

marshal, marshall — The first is the verb or the noun — to *marshal* your forces, or be a parade or a fire *marshal.* The second is a person's name: actor E.G. Marshall, Gen. George Marshall.

militate, mitigate — To *militate* (with the preposition against) means to have weight or an effect against. To *mitigate* means to ease or soften.

ongoing, continuing — *Ongoing,* like *upcoming,* is a cliché. It's better to say *continuing, progressing* or *under way.*

oral, verbal — *Oral* means words spoken. *Verbal* may apply to words spoken or written: It means the process of refining ideas into words.

oriented — It's clumsy, a showoff and a cliché. You get such silliness as pleasure-*oriented* tourists and student-*oriented* teachers. And of course they would both like to be in profit-*oriented* businesses.

overly — This pops up everywhere. *Overly complicated* wastes space because it ignores the right word, *overcomplicated.* Another, *overly done,* is overdone, too.

persuade, convince — Either may be followed by an *of* phrase or a *that* clause, but only *per-*

suade may be followed by the infinitive *to*. Right: Friends *persuaded* her to leave. Wrong: Friends *convinced* her to leave. *Persuade* means to argue. *Convince* is to overcome the doubts of, to make somebody feel sure.

premier, premiere — *Premier* is a title for the heads of some governments, such as the Canadian provinces. *Premiere* is a noun meaning the first performance of a play, movie, etc. As an adjective it means the first or leading performer, as in a ballet company.

principal, principle — *Principal* is either a noun meaning the chief person or thing, or an adjective meaning first in rank or importance. *Principle* is a doctrine, a law, a fundamental truth or a guiding code of conduct.

prophecy, prophesy — *Prophecy* (see) is a noun, *prophesy* (sigh) a verb.

proved, proven — *Proved* generally is preferred, but *proven* is all right as an adjective: *a proven oil* reserve.

ravage, ravish — *Ravage* is to destroy violently, ruin, devastate. To *ravish* is to seize or carry away fiercely, or to rape.

rebut, refute — *Rebut* means to present counter-arguments, whether effectively or not. *Refute* means actually to disprove something.

scheme, plan — *Scheme* is often a loaded word that suggest deviousness. Stick to *plan* — unless you mean a "secret or underhanded plot."

serve, service — Both can be verbs meaning to provide a service, but be careful. People are *served.* Things and systems that are maintained are *serviced.* So is a mare by a stud.

specialist, expert — The *specialist* simply specializes in a field or professional work. The *expert* is exceptionally skilled and has much training and knowledge in the field. *Expert* is becoming a cliché — or at least overused. Usually the person you describe is a *specialist* who in time may or may not reach *expert* status.

spell out, detail — *Spell out* is a cliché, in the sense of explaining or detailing. Instead, use *detail, explain* or *specify* (and never *spell out in detail*).

stationary, stationery — If it's *stationary*, it's still. A way to remember: If it's *stationery*, you use it to write to someone.

take, bring — *Take* it away. *Bring* it here.

target, concentrate — As a verb, *target* is tired military jargon. Instead, *concentrate, aim at, set a goal* or *set a target.*

that, which — Here's a good guideline: *Which* clauses take commas and *that* clauses don't. If the sentence works without the clause, it's a *which* clause with commas before and after it. If the sentence doesn't work without the clause, it's a *that* clause and takes no commas.

Both of these sentences are correct; "You may borrow the lawnmower, *which* needs gas, for the day" (the sentence works without "*which* needs gas"). "You may borrow the lawnmower *that* is in the garage" (the sentence requires "*that* is in the garage" to distinguish between two mowers, one of which is in the garage). But even though it's correct as written, you don't need *that* at all. Just say: "You may borrow the lawnmower in the garage."

thrust, gist — *Thrust* is a showy noun, suggesting of power, hinting of sex and the darling of executives, politicians and speech writers. It's also a cliché. Use instead *the point, the essence, the force, the main idea* or *the gist. Thrust* is a fine verb but a bad noun.

transpire, happen — *Transpire* is not synonymous for *happen.* People use it because it sounds elegant. Use *happen* or *occur.*

try — You must try *to* do this or that, not try *and* do it.

trigger, set off — As a verb, *trigger* is a cliché (and people are too quick on it — a worse cliché). Any of these substitutes is better: *set off, touch off, start, fire.*

unique — It stands alone; there's no such thing as *very* unique or *rather* unique or *quite* unique or *somewhat* unique. But unless you're sure it's one of a kind, don't use *unique.* Call it *unusual* or *rare.*

unprecedented, unusual — *Unprecedented* is a loaded word. All too often there is a precedent but you're unaware of it. *Unusual* or *rare* are better and safer.

usage, use, utilize — *Usage* means habitual or preferred practice in grammar, law, manners, diplomacy, etc. *Use* is right in referring to employment of an object or consumption of a commodity: the *use* of alcohol, drug *use*, new *uses* of energy, etc. *Utilize* has become a cliché. Some people think it sounds elegant, but competent writers prefer *use*.

who, whom — A tough one. Generally, you're safe to use *whom* to refer to the object of an action and *who* for the one taking the action. *Who* kicked the ball, and to *whom* did he kick it? Or, use *who* whenever you could substitute *he*, *she*, *they*, *I* or *we*. And use *whom* whenever you could substitute *him*, *her*, *them*, *me* or *us*.

wise — As a suffix, use it only in a handful of instances: *clockwise*, *lengthwise*, *otherwise*. Don't use it to make clichés: *profitwise*, *timewise*, *energywise*, *moneywise*, *healthwise*, etc.

REWRITING & EDITING

GOOD WRITERS REWRITE AGAIN AND AGAIN, working on the flow and rhythm of their prose. They know the innards of the words they use. They rewrite, and it shows.

You rewrite to shorten, sharpen, simplify and clarify, to improve order and logic, to examine everything from the reader's point of view. As you rewrite, ask yourself these questions:

- ✍ Have I used verbs in the active voice?
- ✍ Have I placed my subjects close to their verbs?
- ✍ Have I chosen the words that express my meaning precisely?
- ✍ Have I avoided long, difficult sentences?
- ✍ Have I cut out needless words, especially modifiers?
- ✍ Have I avoided sudden shifts in tone — from conversational to fussy, from relaxed to formal?

One trick in rewriting is to sleep on what you have written, then attack it afresh: What you're proud of today may embarrass you tomorrow. Samuel Johnson understood. "Read over your compositions," he said, "and when you meet a passage which you think is particularly fine, strike it out."

Writer Kurt Vonnegut says about the same thing: Have the guts to cut it out. "Your eloquence should be the servant of the ideas in your head," he said. "Your rule might be this: If a sentence, no matter how excellent, does not illuminate your subject in some new and useful way, scratch it out."

(Sometimes that's hard to do. In Chapter 2, about how to talk to your reader, I contrived some advice leading to this line: "Clarity begins at home." It added nothing to my point, so I cut it out.)

When you think you've finished rewriting, run your document through Grammatik again, even though you've done it once already. Don't automatically ignore its every suggestion. Instead, consider comments like "passive voice" or "long sentence" a chance to edit yourself ruthlessly. Is there an alternative to the way you're discussing your topic? As you edit, examine everything from the reader's point of view, make sure nothing is left out, check for accuracy and try to shorten, sharpen, improve and simplify.

Ask yourself these questions:

- ✍ **Are things in order?** Does the reader recognize my beginning, my middle and my end? Have I given the reader a clear, well-marked trail? Does everything follow logically?
- ✍ **Am I clear?** Could I be less abstract, more down-to-earth?
- ✍ **How is my tone?** In trying to be conversational, have I been too "talky" and chummy? Too formal? Rude? Sympathetic?
- ✍ **Do my attempts at humor work?** If a light touch, a play on words or a funny story seem to fit, fine. But if you have any doubts, forget it. Humor that misses really misses.

A sense of humor helps — both about what you write and about yourself. Nat Schmulowitz was a simple man, a lawyer-historian-writer. He concluded that people's humor can be more interesting than straight histories, and tell as much about them. He wrote:

"A vain man, a bigoted man, or an angry man cannot laugh at himself, or be laughed at. But the man who can laugh at himself, or be laughed at, has taken another step toward the perfect sanity that brings peace on earth and good will toward man."

Enough. It was hard work and you're done. But there's one more step. Show your writing to some people you respect and see what you overlooked. Then rewrite.

USE EVERY ADVANTAGE

WE ESTABLISH THE BOUNDARIES of our world to help us make decisions about change. In my 40 years in journalism, I've seen a revolution in the tools available to help us write. I've also met a lot of writers who have said things like "I'll never need a computer — I've always written this way," and "Writing is writing. Machines make it faster, not better."

It's tragic, because these people cut themselves off from tools that could free them to be more creative in their work. They also narrow their perspective on the world around them, and that means that what they write is dated. Some of the most useful electronic writing tools available now include:

- ✍ word processor
- ✍ outliner
- ✍ spelling checker
- ✍ electronic thesaurus
- ✍ grammar and style checker

My favorite is Grammatik, which checks my work for grammar and style errors. I love being able to customize its proofreading. That means I'm not tied to arcane rules of writing, and my proofreading is done quickly and thoroughly. Many of the style and grammar suggestions in this book are built into Grammatik.

Which of these tools are necessary for successful writing? All of them. They will help you work faster and produce writing that is more accurate and readable. Which brings me to the point: Successful writing is readable writing. Use every advantage you can get (even computers) to make your writing readable. That's all.

SUMMARY

"EVERY SUCCESSFUL PIECE OF NONFICTION should leave the reader with one provocative thought he (or she) didn't have before," William Zinsser advises. "Not two thoughts, or five—just one...." He's right. I believe several of my guidelines are more important than the others — even provocative — but all 20 add up to one point: Simple, conversational language results in clear writing.

To make a point, other writers suggest making it three times: Tell people what you're going to tell them, tell them, then tell them what you've told them. So here, in brief, is what I have told you about the way to clear writing:

- **Respect your readers.** Fix an assortment of people in your mind and write for them — with respect.
- **Think it through.** You must first have a plan that gives you a beginning, a middle and an end.
- **"Talk" to your readers**—with simple, honest and conversational language.
- **Stick to the simple sentence,** with one main idea for each one—generally—but vary the length for good rhythm.
- **Be specific and precise.** Don't tell, don't explain — show.
- **Be brief,** but you get brevity by selection, not just by compression.
- **Move your readers along.** Don't just stack the facts; try to tell a story.

- ✍ **People writing works best.** It means writing *about* people and *to* people by involving them.
- ✍ **When in doubt, punctuate.** When not don't. And use the period often.
- ✍ **Become an activist** and unsmother the verbs hidden in nouns.
- ✍ **Adverbs are redundant** and waste words, terribly.
- ✍ **Adjectives,** too, are a terrible waste.
- ✍ **Loaded words** are unfair and, besides, they tell on you.
- ✍ **Clichés** make people laugh *at* you, not *with* you.
- ✍ **Metaphors and similes** enrich the language, until you scramble them or until they become clichés. Then people laugh at you.
- ✍ **Jargon and vogue words** embarrass us, or should. Literate people avoid these show-offs.
- ✍ **Even one little slip** can reveal a writer who's uncomfortable with the language.
- ✍ **To fight clutter,** make every word work.
- ✍ **Even the good words** can hurt you if you misuse or confuse them.
- ✍ **Rewrite, edit yourself ruthlessly and rewrite**. Then proofread again.

Finally, don't sabotage yourself by closing your mind to innovation. When you set out to write, you set out to communicate. Use every tool you can to do it well.

MORE WRITING HELP